Sponges

Meryl Magby

PowerKiDS
press.
New York

For Riley Grace Parker, my adorable goddaughter

Published in 2013 by The Rosen Publishing Group, Inc.
29 East 21st Street, New York, NY 10010

First Edition

Editor: Jennifer Way
Book Design: Greg Tucker

Photo Credits: Cover, pp. 4, 5, 6, 7, 8, 9, 10, 12–13, 14, 16 Shutterstock.com; p. 11 © www.iStockphoto.com/Mehmet Hilmi Barcin; pp. 15 Daniela Dirscheri/WaterFrame/Getty Images; p. 17 Bill Curtsinger/National Geographic/Getty Images; pp. 18—19 Reinhard Dirscheri/WaterFrame/Getty Images; p. 20 Borut Furlan/WaterFrame/Getty Images; p. 21 Ethan Daniels/WaterFrame/Getty Images; p. 22 Hemera/Thinkstock.

Library of Congress Cataloging-in-Publication Data

Magby, Meryl.
 Sponges / by Meryl Magby. — 1st ed.
    p. cm. — (Under the sea)
 ISBN 978-1-4488-7399-9 (library binding) — ISBN 978-1-4488-7478-1 (pbk.) —
ISBN 978-1-4488-7552-8 (6-pack)
 1. Sponges—Juvenile literature. I. Title.
 QL371.6.M34 2013
 593.4—dc23

                          2011047760

Manufactured in the United States of America

CPSIA Compliance Information: Batch #WKTS12PK: For Further Information contact Rosen Publishing, New York, New York at 1-800-237-9932

Contents

Meet the Sea Sponge

Sea sponges are amazing underwater animals. People thought sponges were plants until the 1700s. This may be because they do not seem to move. However, sponges are the oldest living animals on Earth.

Sponges are animals in the **phylum** called Porifera. These animals **evolved** in early prehistoric times.

Yellow tube sponges, shown here, live throughout the Caribbean Sea and in the Gulf of Mexico.

4

This is a barrel sponge growing in the Indian Ocean near the island of Bali, in Indonesia.

Today, scientists have found more than 5,000 **species** of sponges. However, they think there may be up to 15,000 living species of sponges.

Do you know the cartoon character SpongeBob Squarepants? In real life, sponges are nothing like SpongeBob! Sponges are like water filters in the ocean. They pump huge amounts of water through their bodies each day.

Living Underwater

Sponges live in underwater **habitats** all over the world. Most sponges are found in Earth's oceans and seas. However, some sponges live in freshwater habitats, such as lakes.

Sponges can live in every depth of water. Some sponges live in very shallow water along the coast. Others live in the deepest parts of the open ocean.

Many sponges live among coral reefs. These habitats are often full of fish and other ocean life.

Top: These red tube sponges are living in the warm, shallow water of the Caribbean Sea near the coast of Panama. *Right:* The red boring sponge can be red, orange, or yellow. It is a widespread sponge that attaches itself to some kinds of sea animals.

Adult sponges stay attached to hard objects. Sponges may attach themselves to the ocean floor or to the tops of rocks, shells, corals, or even other underwater animals.

Sponges are very common in warm tropical waters. Many species of sponges live among tropical coral reefs and sea grasses.

Many Shapes and Colors

Sponges come in many different shapes, sizes, and colors. Tropical sponges are often very brightly colored. Some sponges' bodies are shaped like trees, fans, cups, tubes, vases, or balls. Others are shapeless. Sponges range from a few millimeters to more than 6 feet (2 m) long.

This vase sponge has a wide opening at the top and narrows toward its bottom. It has brittle stars crawling on it.

Stovepipe sponges form long, purple-gray tubes.

Sponges are **invertebrates**. This means they do not have backbones. Instead, sponges' bodies are held together with skeletons made from stretchy fibers and hard minerals. The top layer of sponges' bodies is covered with small holes, called pores. Water passes through the pores into passageways than run through sponges' bodies.

The Oldest Animal

Fossils show that sponges are Earth's oldest organisms with more than one cell. They evolved over 600 million years ago. Scientists think that the sponge species living today are not very different from prehistoric sponges. This is why they are sometimes called living fossils. Some scientists even think that the sponge is the one animal that all other animals evolved from!

The sponges living today are not much different from those that lived millions of years ago.

Fossils of sponges are found all over the world. Because Earth has changed over millions of years, many places where the fossils are found are no longer near the ocean!

Prehistoric sponges covered the ocean floor. As sponges were the earliest animals, they did not have many **predators** for a long time. This means they could grow and evolve new species very easily.

Sponge Facts

1 Sponges belong to the phylum Porifera. The name "Porifera" means "pore-having" in Latin.

2 Unlike most other animals, sponges do not have organs or tissues. Instead, sponges' bodies are made up of different kinds of special cells.

3 Sponges cam pump four to five times their volume of water through their bodies in 1 minute. A sponge's volume is the measure of space that its body takes up.

4 Sponges often have names that tell you what they look like. The orange puffball sponge looks like a puffy orange ball! The velvety red sponge looks like soft red velvet.

5 Sponges are very good at filtering, or removing, small organisms called bacteria from water. Sponges remove 90 percent of the bacteria from the water that passes through their bodies.

6 When dinosaurs roamed Earth, a giant glass sponge reef stretched across the ocean where Europe is today.

7 Sponges work hard to filter food from the water they pump through their bodies. When they filter 1 ton (1 t) of water through their bodies, they take in only 1 ounce (28 g) of food.

8 The sponges in one family catch and eat small animals called crustaceans. The crustaceans get stuck on the sponges' skeletons!

9 Hermit sponges travel on the backs of hermit crabs. The sponge attaches itself to a snail shell. Then a hermit crab uses the shell as its home.

Sponges in Reefs

Most sponges live in large groups in their ocean habitats. These groups are called colonies. Sponge colonies often live in coral reefs. They are an important part of the reef habitat. They help the plants and other animals that live there. Sponges make **nutrients** that help coral and algae grow. Sponges can also

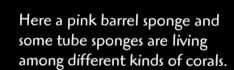

Here a pink barrel sponge and some tube sponges are living among different kinds of corals.

Fish sometimes hide among sponges. Here, a tasseled scorpion fish hides inside a barrel sponge as it hunts for other fish to eat.

give small ocean animals places to hide from predators. However, sponges are not always good neighbors. Sometimes they drill holes in the corals and mollusks to which they are attached.

Adult sponges generally do not move. However, scientists have found that some sponges can move up to .15 inch (4 mm) a day.

How Sponges Eat

No other animals eat as sponges do. Sponges do not have mouths! Instead, they have special systems that let water flow through their bodies. The water gives them food and **oxygen**. It also carries out their waste.

In this photograph, you can see the tiny pores through which water flows into the sponge's body. Water flows out of the sponge through the larger holes.

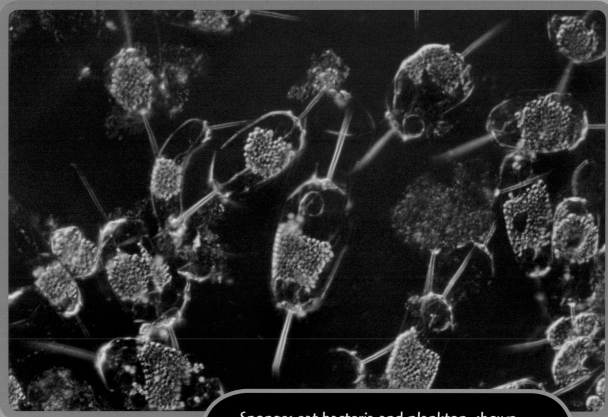

Sponges eat bacteria and plankton, shown here. Plankton are tiny, floating plants and animals that live in the world's oceans.

First, water passes into the sponges' bodies through tiny pores. Special cells use tiny whiplike parts to move water through passageways in the sponges' bodies. The sponges then filter tiny animals, such as bacteria and plankton, from the water. Bacteria and plankton are food for sponges. Finally, the water travels out of the sponges' bodies through larger holes.

Sponges reproduce, or make more sponges, in two different ways. Some sponge species can reproduce by themselves. They grow new sponges as buds on their bodies.

Other sponge species reproduce with the help of other sponges. Most of these sponges make both **sperm** and eggs. First they send their sperm into the water. Then the sperm **fertilizes** eggs inside other sponges. The eggs grow into **larvae**. The sponge lets out the larvae. Then the larvae attach to something hard. There they grow into young sponges.

Here is a sponge releasing larvae.

Predators and Poisons

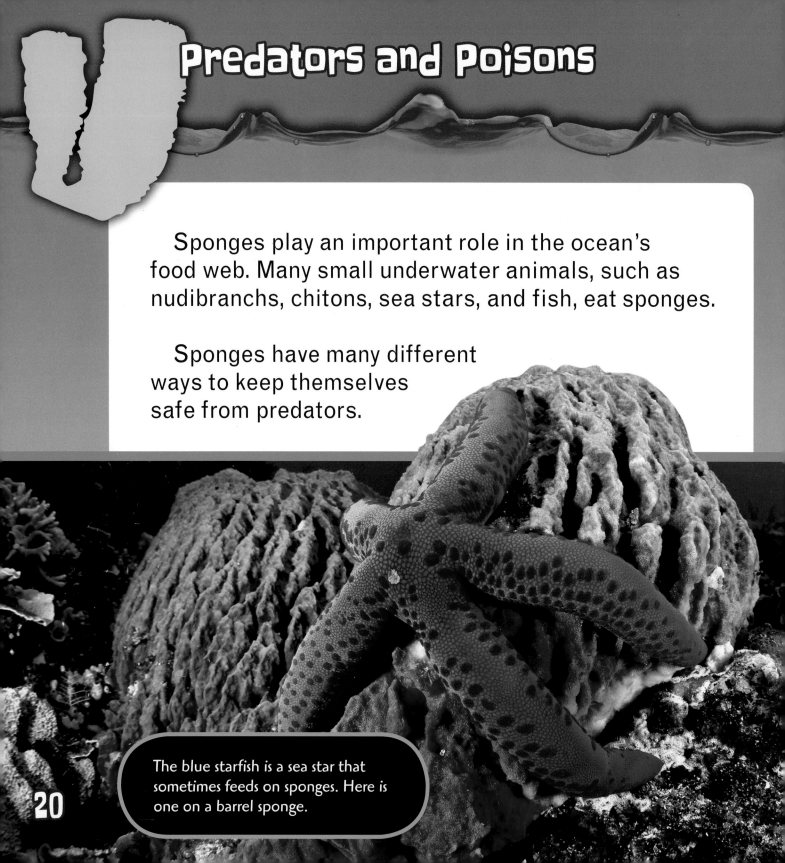

Sponges play an important role in the ocean's food web. Many small underwater animals, such as nudibranchs, chitons, sea stars, and fish, eat sponges.

Sponges have many different ways to keep themselves safe from predators.

The blue starfish is a sea star that sometimes feeds on sponges. Here is one on a barrel sponge.

Nudibranchs are sluglike invertebrates that live in the ocean. The ones shown here are grazing on a red sponge.

Sponges make poisonous chemicals that keep most other animals from eating them. These chemicals also keep sponges safe from other sponges that want to attach to them.

Sponges can also keep safe from predators by living in deep, dark places. Sponges that live deep in coral reefs are often safe from predators.

Keeping Sponges Safe

In parts of the world, some sponge species are in danger. Many people like to use sea sponges as bath sponges. However, too

These are natural sponges for sale. It is a good idea to look for sponges that are grown and picked in ways that do not hurt the ocean environment and that help the economy in the places where sponges are grown.

many sponges are being cut and sold. Soon, these wild sponges may be gone.

People can buy sea sponges that were raised **sustainably**. This means that sponges are not cut faster than the populations can regrow. It is important to make choices that keep a healthy balance of plant and animal life in the world's oceans.

Glossary

evolved (ih-VOLVD) Changed over many years.

fertilizes (FUR-tuh-lyz-ez) Puts male cells inside eggs to make babies.

fossils (FO-sulz) The hardened remains of dead animals or plants.

habitats (HA-buh-tats) The places where animals or plants naturally live.

invertebrates (in-VER-teh-brets) Animals without backbones.

larvae (LAHR-vee) Animals in an early period of life.

nutrients (NOO-tree-ents) Food that a living thing needs to live and grow.

oxygen (OK-sih-jen) A gas that has no color or taste and is necessary for people and animals to breathe.

phylum (FY-lum) One of the main parts of the animal kingdom.

predators (PREH-duh-terz) Animals that kill other animals for food.

species (SPEE-sheez) One kind of living thing. All people are one species.

sperm (SPERM) A special male cell that, with a female egg, can make a baby.

sustainably (suh-STAY-nuh-blee) Done in a way that allows something to be kept going.

Index

Websites

Due to the changing nature of Internet links, PowerKids Press has developed an online list of websites related to the subject of this book. This site is updated regularly. Please use this link to access the list: www.powerkidslinks.com/uts/spon/